The Awesome Autistic Go-To Guide

by the same author

**The Parents' Practical Guide to Resilience for
Preteens and Teenagers on the Autism Spectrum**
Jeanette Purkis and Emma Goodall
ISBN 978 1 78592 275 6
eISBN 978 1 78450 575 2

**The Parents' Practical Guide to Resilience for
Children aged 2–10 on the Autism Spectrum**
Jeanette Purkis and Emma Goodall
ISBN 978 1 78592 274 9
eISBN 978 1 78450 574 5

The Guide to Good Mental Health on the Autism Spectrum
Jeanette Purkis, Emma Goodall and Jane Nugent
Forewords by Wenn Lawson and Kirsty Dempster-Rivett
ISBN 978 1 84905 670 0
eISBN 978 1 78450 195 2

The Wonderful World of Work
A Workbook for Asperteens
Jeanette Purkis
Illustrated by Andrew Hore
ISBN 978 1 84905 499 7
eISBN 978 0 85700 923 4

of related interest

You Can Change the World!
Everyday Teen Heroes Making a Difference Everywhere
Margaret Rooke
Forewords by Taylor Richardson and Katie Hodgetts
Illustrated by Kara McHale
ISBN 978 1 78592 502 3
eISBN 978 1 78450 897 5

Know Your Spectrum!
An Autism Creative Writing Workbook for Teens
Finn Monahan
ISBN 978 1 78592 435 4

The Asperkid's (Secret) Book of Social Rules
**The Handbook of Not-So-Obvious Social Guidelines for
Tweens and Teens with Asperger Syndrome**
Jennifer Cook O'Toole
Illustrated by Brian Bojanowski
ISBN 978 1 84905 915 2
eISBN 978 0 85700 685 1

THE AWESOME AUTISTIC GO-TO GUIDE

A Practical Handbook for Autistic Teens and Tweens

Yenn Purkis and **Tanya Masterman**

Illustrated by Glynn Masterman

Foreword by Dr Emma Goodall

Jessica Kingsley Publishers
London and Philadelphia

First published in 2020
by Jessica Kingsley Publishers
73 Collier Street
London N1 9BE, UK
and
400 Market Street, Suite 400
Philadelphia, PA 19106, USA

www.jkp.com

Copyright © Yenn Purkis and Tanya Masterman 2020
Illustrations copyright © Glynn Masterman 2020
Foreword copyright © Dr Emma Goodall 2020

Library of Congress Cataloging in Publication Data
A CIP catalog record for this book is available from the Library of Congress

British Library Cataloguing in Publication Data
A CIP catalogue record for this book is available from the British Library

ISBN 978 1 78775 316 7
eISBN 978 1 78775 317 4

Printed and bound in Great Britain

*For my daughter, Samara, who has taught
me more than I could ever teach her.
Tanya*

*To all of the autistic kids and teens. You deserve pride and
the knowledge that you are amazing just as you are.
Yenn*

Contents

Foreword by Dr Emma Goodall 9

1. All About Autism 11

2. Introducing Some Other Amazing People
   Who Are a Bit Like You 25

3. Why You Just Might Be Awesome. 39

4. Why Being You Can Sometimes Be Hard . . 51

5. Some Ways to Make Life Easier 63

6. Growing Up True to You 85

7. Telling Others About Your Autism 93

8. Big Yay for Being You! 99

Foreword

Dr Emma Goodall

I wish that all books for young people were as helpful and informative as this practical handbook for autistic teens and tweens. When I realized that I learnt more easily when I was interested, I thought I was strange; some people thought I was lazy. But as an autistic adult I became fascinated with autism and have been researching autism for nearly 10 years, and I have learnt that our brains are organized in ways that mean we learn best when we are interested.

I have known and connected with the authors of this book in a number of different ways for nearly a decade. Both are committed to and passionate about helping other autistics live life and achieve their dreams, whether through mentoring, public speaking or writing.

This book will help autistic young people find and develop the confidence to be who they are and find strategies to help them live life with as little stress as possible and be the best autistic they can be. My passions are helping people to live the best life they can. A good life means having purpose and being connected, whether to other people or places or animals or music or something else, but always to self.

So, my tip for readers is to learn about yourself from the inside out. This book will be a great help, and, as it was written by autistic adults, it won't be making suggestions that don't make sense or won't be of any use!

Getting to know yourself really well sounds strange, but when you connect to and know your 'self' really well, your interoception improves and you can manage your emotions and the world around you more easily. I love that I can now manage my emotions much better through practising interoception every day.

If you want to know more about interoception, have a look at my YouTube channel www.youtube.com/channel/UCylovxevV3W2l2WXHDBkKxA

Dr Emma Goodall
Healthy Possibilities
www.healthypossibilities.net
Mindful Body Awareness
www.mindfulbodyawareness.com

Chapter 1

All About Autism

Hi! If you're autistic, this book is for you. We, the authors of this book, are autistic too. So are lots of other interesting people. This book is all about being autistic – what it might feel like and some of the good things autistic people can do. It has some tips for managing tricky situations and reasons why being you can be totally awesome! This is your book for getting to know yourself and your autism. It has lots of useful information and fascinating facts about autism. There are some fun activities and places where you can write in your thoughts. You may already know some things about autism or you might not know much. Whichever way, this book will help you to understand more about who you are and what it means to be autistic.

In this book, you will see a few cartoons with stick figures. Some of the stick figures have heads with 'Au' written in them. They represent autistic people. The stick figures with plain heads represent non-autistic people.

ACTIVITY: What do you think about autism?

You might have only just discovered you are autistic, or you may have known for some time. You probably have some thoughts about autism and being autistic. Write down up to 10 things that you think of when you think, see, or hear the word 'autism'. There are no right or wrong answers — just write down what comes into your mind.

1. ....

....

2. ....

....

3. ....

....

4. ....

....

5. ....

....

6. ....

....

7. ....

....

8. ....

....

9. ....

....

10. ....

....

TALKING ABOUT AUTISM – AM I AUTISTIC OR DO I HAVE AUTISM?

People talk differently about autism. Some people say 'I'm autistic', some say 'I have autism', 'I'm on the spectrum' or 'I'm an autie', or something else. It's totally your choice how you talk about your autism and you. This book uses 'I am autistic', but it is up to you how you choose to describe yourself. It might take a while to work out how you want to talk about your autism. That is perfectly okay, and there is no rush. You can work it out in your own time.

DOING THINGS DIFFERENTLY

People who are autistic often feel like they are different from other people. In fact, it is often true that they are. There are a lot of things autistic people do differently from people who are not autistic.

Some ways in which autistic people can be different are:

■ We are often very focused on what we are interested in. This can mean we know a LOT about the subject or subjects that we love. We really enjoy thinking about our interests and doing things related to them.

- Our senses usually work differently from other people's. Autistic people often find noises very loud, lights very glary and smells very smelly. Most people who are not autistic do not have such very perceptive senses.

- We feel differently. This means that sometimes we can feel the emotions of other people just by being near them. It also means that sometimes it can be hard to know what we are feeling. When we do feel an emotion, it can be very 'big' and can take us by surprise.

- We understand people differently. People who are not autistic can often understand what someone is feeling or thinking by looking at the expression on their face and how they move their body and the 'tone' of their voice. Often, autistic people are not able to notice or understand these things.

- Autistic people are almost always very honest. We do not usually need to make any effort to tell the truth — we do it anyway! People who are not autistic often have a different idea of what honesty means. This can be confusing for us and sometimes for them as well!

There is nothing wrong or bad about being different. In fact, being different can be a very good thing!

DION IS DIFFERENT

Dion is very tall. He is different from other kids in his class because he is a lot taller. Dion likes being tall, though, as it means he can reach higher than everyone else and he is great at sports where being tall helps, like basketball and netball.

ELLIE IS DIFFERENT

Ellie is different because she can draw really beautiful pictures of characters from *Star Wars*, which is her favourite thing in the world. Ellie knows a LOT of things about the *Star Wars* universe. Her drawings are so good that when she gives them to other people for a birthday present they say a big 'thank you' and comment on how lovely her art is. Drawing *Star Wars* pictures makes Ellie really happy. Ellie is autistic.

KY IS DIFFERENT

Ky is different because they have an amazing memory. Ky can remember everyone's birthday and even what day of the week friends and family members were born on. Ky is also very good at maths and can do complicated calculations in their mind. A lot of people think Ky's difference is very cool indeed. Ky is autistic as well.

GOOD THINGS ABOUT DIFFERENCE

A different way of looking at the world

Having people in the world who are different from one another is a really positive thing. It is important to have a variety of ways of looking at the world. Different ways of thinking and doing things make it possible for us to have a world where not everyone and everything is the same. If everyone thought and acted the same way, humans would be like robots. There would be no new solutions to problems, no creativity and no interesting art, drama or music. Life would be very boring indeed!

BEING AUTISTIC

As an autistic person you are far from alone. Lots of other kids are autistic and many adults are too. There may be some other autistic people in your family or at your school. You may have some friends who are autistic too.

WHAT IS AUTISM?

Autism means that your brain is 'wired' in a different way to non-autistic people's brains. Your brain works differently from other people's brains. Being autistic is as much a part of you as having the colour of hair that you have or the shape of your nose. It is something you were born with and which will always be a part of you.

Autistic people often have a number of experiences that most non-autistic people do not have. These include things like:

- Being very focused

- Absolutely loving a topic – this is sometimes called a 'special interest' or a 'passionate interest'

- Having very strong reactions to sounds, textures, light, smells and tastes

- Having a quirky sense of humour

- Loving words and making jokes related to words (called 'puns' or 'word play')

- Being very uncomfortable when people make eye contact with you

- Sometimes needing time alone in a quiet space

- Noticing things that other people do not, like patterns in numbers

- Not always wanting to play with other kids

- Finding new things and change stressful

- Being frightened or worried about things non-autistic people do not even notice

- Stimming – this means doing things like flapping your hands or using a fidget toy, which helps you de-stress and feel good

- Feeling very close to animals and being able to understand them.

WHAT DOES IT NOT MEAN TO BE AUTISTIC?

Some people have thoughts and beliefs about autism that are wrong. These wrong beliefs include thinking that:

- Autistic people do not have any emotions

- Autistic people don't care about other people and have no empathy

- Autistic kids are being deliberately 'naughty' when they aren't

- All autistic people are violent

- Autistic people cannot use their imaginations

■ There is a different person 'hiding' or 'trapped' under their autism.

If people say any of these things, it means that they do not know very much about autism and autistic people.

All autistic people are different from one another, just like everyone else. Being autistic is not the only way to describe you. It is a very important part of you, but it is not the only thing that makes you who you are. You might be very funny. You might have super-flexible thumbs. You might be very interested in and care deeply about endangered animals. You might be awesome at building rollercoasters in Minecraft.

Being autistic is not 'good' or 'bad' – it simply means that people think differently. There are usually some very good bits and some not so good bits to being autistic.

FRIENDS HAVE THINGS IN COMMON

Every single person in the world is a little bit different and this is true for autistic people too. People are often friends with others who share something in common with them. This might be an interest or a fandom. Their families might be from the same country or they might live in the same street. It is very common that autistic people make friends with other autistic people. Autistic kids – and adults too – often make friends with other autistic people because autistic people tend to have a lot of things in common. Now you know that you are autistic, it might mean that you meet other autistic people that you have things in common with and you might become friends with them.

Friends share interests

So now you know more about what autism is and why being different is not a bad thing, but an important part of how the world works. Here is a space where you can write down your thoughts and any questions you thought of while reading Chapter 1, if you want to.

ACTIVITY: My thoughts, questions and comments on Chapter 1, All About Autism

1. ....

   ....

2. ....

   ....

3. ....

   ....

4. ....

   ....

5. ....

   ....

6. ....

   ....

7. ....

   ....

8. ....

   ....

9. ....

   ....

10. ....

   ....

In the next chapter you will meet some other people and characters who are a bit like you.

Chapter 2

Introducing Some Other Amazing People Who Are a Bit Like You

Just like we said in Chapter 1, every single person in the world is different. This means that you won't be the same as every other autistic person you meet, or every other person in your family, or every other person who likes some of the things you do. This chapter talks about some other people who are autistic – just like you. You might have things in common with some of them.

Some of the people are real and some are characters from TV shows, films or books. Some people from history might have been autistic too, but we can't really tell for sure. Some people think physicist Albert Einstein was autistic, and artist Leonardo da Vinci and music composer Wolfgang

Amadeus Mozart. Most autistic people do not have those kinds of 'genius' skills.

Autistic people can be experts in what we are very interested in, because our passion gives us lots of focus and motivation to learn and create. So, we might learn everything there is to know about one topic and discover more things about it as well. Some people call our passions 'special interests', but we think that sounds a bit silly. They're not 'special' – they're just things that we really like and have a strong passion for.

REAL PEOPLE WHO ARE AUTISTIC

Satoshi Tajiri

You might have heard of Satoshi. He is the Japanese game designer who invented Pokémon! When he was a boy, insect collecting was his passion. Then, when he was a teenager, he really loved video games. School was tricky, and he nearly didn't finish high school. When he was in his late teens, he wrote and edited a gamer magazine called *Game Freak*, with tips for gamers. That led Satoshi to realize that lots of games really weren't designed that well, and that he'd like to try designing his own.

He had the idea for Pokémon in 1990. By then, many areas of Japan had been covered in concrete and there weren't as many places to hunt live bugs, so Satoshi found another way – in a game! People all over the world love Pokémon. Maybe you have an amazing imagination and invent new games and characters in your mind too.

Carly Fleischmann

Can you host a talk show if you can't talk? Sure you can! Carly does. She is a Canadian woman who is autistic and has something called oral motor apraxia. These are just big words for having problems getting speech messages from your brain to your mouth, so words don't come out. It's great that we live in a time where there is so much technology around to use to enable people to communicate if they don't speak out loud.

Carly is a media presenter. She uses text-to-speech (TTS) technology to interview her guests. She just types her questions onto her computer, which then reads them out in her chosen voice. Her show is called *Speechless* and she's very funny. Her first guest was Channing Tatum – you might have heard of him!

There are plenty of autistic people who communicate in ways other than verbal speech. They might use other sounds, or pictures, or sign language, or assistive technology. These kinds of communication are just as good as using your voice, as Carly's experience shows.

James Durbin

James Durbin is an American singer and musician who was once on *American Idol*; he then released some of his own albums. For two years, he was the lead singer for a band called Quiet Riot, which has been around a long time, even when we (the authors of this book) were teenagers! James is now doing music of his own, like an acoustic show.

James is autistic and also has something called Tourette's. People who have Tourette's have 'tics'. A tic is an unusual movement or sound that a person has little or no control over.

Music is James's passion, and he feels most at home on stage when he can just be himself. James has said that autism has helped him to really focus and be involved in what he loves.

Some of James's songs are about his experiences of being autistic, including some really tough ones. Music is a great way to work through difficult emotions. Perhaps you play an instrument, sing or like listening to music. Or maybe you feel music very deeply.

I am Cadence

Cadence is an Australian girl who loves art and writing. She uses sign language, writing and forms of communication other than talking. When she was only seven, her first piece of published writing, 'Autism is Why I am Different', was made into a short film, called *Acceptance*. She also sells some of her artwork on the art website Redbubble.[1]

Cadence really loves animals and being outside. Lots of autistic people connect strongly with nature. Maybe you do too.

She has some very interesting things to say, like:

I don't like it when people say I'm special. Special is an adjective. It means better or greater. I'm not better than other people. I'm not more important than my friends. Autism doesn't make me special. It just makes me different. I'm good at some things. I'm not good at other things, just like everyone else.[2]

The AutistiX

Jack, Luke and Saul, three of the six band members from The AutistiX, are, you guessed it, autistic! The AutistiX is a rock band from a place called Camden, in London. They met at a meet-up for musicians

---

1 See www.redbubble.com; you can find Cadence's work at www.iamcadence.com

2 I am Cadence (2016) 'Autism doesn't make me special.' I am Cadence – Autism Through a Child's Eyes, 7 May. Available at https://iamcadence.com/2016/05/07/autism-doesnt-make-me-special/ (accessed on 18 May 2019).

with disabilities and decided to form a band with a few other people.

The AutistiX use their music to help them express themselves socially in ways they can find hard at other times. Their first music video, released a few years ago, was called 'Just the Same' and is a song about inclusion and acceptance. You can find it on YouTube — it's worth a listen and you can tell how much fun they're having making music together, smiling and laughing.[3]

Stephen Wiltshire

Some autistic people have what is called a splinter skill, when they are absolutely amazing at one thing. Sometimes it's also called a savant skill. Stephen Wiltshire is one of those people. He's an architectural artist from England and he draws very detailed pictures of entire cities from his memory. He does things like taking a flight in a helicopter over a city, remembering what he sees and then drawing or painting it. He started drawing very detailed buildings when he was seven and he started talking when he was nine. His autism gives him a very deep passion for buildings and cityscapes, which helps him in his work.

---

3   See www.youtube.com/watch?v=ilytN26el1Q

Summer Farrelly

Chickens act a bit like people

Summer is an Australian girl who invented a therapy programme called 'Chickens to Love'. She loves chickens and, by carefully watching their behaviour, she noticed their interesting social structure. She thought they acted a bit like people, because they have friendship groups, they don't all like each other and behave like people in other ways too. Summer feels other people's emotions and sometimes that's hard. Watching the chickens has helped her learn about and understand how people act.

Summer's programme 'Chickens to Love' lets other autistic kids take part too!

Dr Wenn Lawson

Dr Wenn Lawson is a British autistic psychologist and has been travelling around the world, talking about autism, for 25 years. He has also written and contributed to more than 20 books. You could call him an expert on autism, that's for sure! He also talks about gender and knows a lot about that as well.

Wenn says:

> Inclusion isn't about including us all equally it's about including us all differently. It's our differences that add so much colour to the world. It's our differences that place an overview of how something can be seen in a way which gives a project its edge or a meal its flavour.[4]

His favourite thing about being autistic is his ability to focus and connect to things that interest him. That helped him get through his studies at university.[5]

---

4   Lawson, W. (2017) 'The Future, as I Would Like to See It.' Wenn's Thoughts, 2 October. Available at www.wenn.buildsomethingpositive. com

5   You can find Dr Wenn's wisdom at www.buildsomethingpositive. com/wenn

ACTIVITY: See if you can find out about some autistic people who like the same or similar things you do

1. ....

....

2. ....

....

3. ....

....

4. ....

....

5. ....

....

CHARACTERS FROM FICTION WHO ARE AUTISTIC

William 'Billy' Cranston (a Power Ranger)

Billy the Blue Ranger is autistic too. He likes lining things up, like pencils. Lots of autistic people find that sorting things like this is very calming. You might have a collection you like sorting and classifying, like crystals or fossils, or LEGO or coloured pens or buttons. Or maybe chocolates!

Sometimes Billy has trouble understanding sarcastic jokes. Some autistic people find these a challenge. Billy has an excellent memory and is talented at maths and logical thinking. Many autistic people think in a logical way and some are very good at things like maths and coding.

Billy works in a team with the other Power Rangers to save the day.

Maurice Moss (in the TV programme *The IT Crowd*)

Moss works in IT in a comedy show called *The IT Crowd*. Sometimes his work colleagues want him to tell lies to cover up something they have done wrong, but Moss is bad at lying. And that's a good thing! Most autistic people are very honest and always like to tell the truth. Moss likes technology and inventing things, but sometimes they go wrong in a very funny way. Do you ever invent things? It doesn't matter if they don't work; we learn a lot from experiments and can think about what might work better next time.

Wendy (in the film *Please Stand By*)

Wendy's passion is *Star Trek*. She is a teenage girl who has written a script to enter in a screenwriting contest. She accidentally missed the mailing date and decided to deliver the script herself. Her passion gives her the focus and determination to overcome lots of obstacles on her journey to deliver her entry. The film shows some horrible things happening to Wendy, especially at the start. Many people are unkind to her and don't understand her, but she is so determined and passionate that she keeps going and it all works out well in the end, including Wendy outsmarting a very unhelpful, arrogant person. There is a police officer who speaks in Klingon to Wendy – he really 'gets' her. But no more spoilers!

Dr Temperance 'Bones' Brennan (in the TV programme *Bones*)

Dr Brennan (her nickname is 'Bones') is a forensic anthropologist. She works with the FBI and helps to solve crimes by examining bodies. She really loves dolphins and she once had a pet mouse, a snake and some spiders. Autistic people sometimes like to have unusual pets. Do you have any pets?

Sometimes 'Bones' finds it hard to understand why people behave the way they do, and has challenges identifying and explaining her emotions. But she loves the logical detective work she does in her job, all based on science. Her autism helps her to look at evidence in a very logical way.

Gary Bell (in the TV programme Alphas)

Gary is a transducer (that means he can convert energy from one form to another) who can see electromagnetic signals with mind power! That takes sensory sensitivities to a new level! Imagine being able to hack into mobile phone, TV and Wi-Fi signals without any hardware at all. He can detect communication between insects if he is in the forest. He also has what is called 'echolalia', which is when autistic people like saying the same words. They might be words from a song or a TV show, or just words that feel nice in our mouths, like 'quotient' or 'velvet'. Do you have any favourite words to say?

Sometimes Gary feels overwhelmed when he picks up too much data at the same time – a bit like how we can feel in a shopping mall when there is too much noise and light, and too many people and smells.

Luna Lovegood (in the *Harry Potter* books)

Some people think that Luna is autistic. She sees things the other characters don't see, is creative, determined and very good at details. This is common for many autistic people – we sometimes see and remember little things that non-autistic people don't. She is also very kind and caring and enjoys thinking time on her own, like being in the forest feeding the Thestrals. How cool would that be? And lots of autistic kids REALLY love *Harry Potter* so it's good to have a character who is a bit like us in some ways.

So, as you see, there is a huge variety of autistic people out there. You might have things in common with some of them. And some won't be like you at all, except for being autistic. When you think about it, humans are a bit like cats. Cats are all cats but they all look different and have different personalities. Some cats like cuddles and some don't. Some cats like to play with cat toys and some don't. Some cats will let their human friends dress them up in silly clothes and some (probably most) won't! Every single cat is different, but they are all like one another, just like people.

⇌ Chapter 3 ⇋

Why You Just Might Be Awesome

There are some good things and some not so good things about being autistic. A lot of the things that are not so good actually happen because some people are not always very understanding or kind to autistic people. These things are more about other people's poor attitudes and nothing to do with autism at all.

One of the worst things about this sort of thinking is that it means that autistic people are seen – and treated – like we are doing things 'wrong'. Some people think that we need to be 'fixed' and made to act more like non-autistic people. This kind of thinking can mean that we feel bad about ourselves. In fact you – and all the other autistic people in the world – don't need 'fixing' at all. We aren't broken! This chapter is all about the good things about being autistic and why it can be great to be different.

AWESOME THINGS ABOUT BEING 'AWETISTIC'

There are plenty of reasons to think about your autism in a positive way. Even though each autistic person is different, there are a few things that many autistic people are very good at. You might be good at some of these things and not others. Or you may be really good at something that isn't on this list.

Positive things about autism and autistic people include:

- Passionate interests (sometimes called 'special interests'), leading to autistic people being 'experts' in a subject very easily. While each person has their own passionate interests, there are some that many autistic kids and adults share, including:

  - Minecraft

  - Anime

  - *Harry Potter*

o Cats, dogs, guinea pigs, snakes, lizards or other animals

o Space exploration

o *Doctor Who*

o Languages

o Art

o LEGO

o Pokémon

o *Star Wars*

o *Star Trek*

and many, many other things.

- Many autistic adults work or study in an area related to a topic they have a passion for.

- Autistic people often have a great ability to focus. We are excellent at focusing on our work and interests.

- Autistic people are also very good at noticing things that others miss. While someone who is not autistic might see a tree and think, 'Ah, that is a tree', an autistic person might see every beautiful, exquisite detail, like an insect crawling on the bark, a droplet of sap or a leaf about to fall.

- Autistic people – both kids and adults – are often wonderful, loyal and kind friends. We can have lots of empathy for other people.

- We are often very thoughtful and considerate of others. Autistic people can also have a strong sense of justice. We might hate it when things are unfair or when someone is being treated badly. People who have these qualities are usually very kind and caring human beings.

- We often have a strong love for nature and a connection with animals, which means we are often great at caring for our pets. Lots of autistic people have a strong bond with animals and feel happy and relaxed when spending time with them.

- We are often very creative. Creativity covers all sorts of things, including art, music and writing, and also coding, design, engineering and science.

Autistic people often see every exquisite detail

ACTIVITY: Do you have any skills or abilities that aren't listed? What are they?

1. ....

....

2. ....

....

3. ....

....

4. . . . .

. . . .

5. . . . .

. . . .

6. . . . .

. . . .

7. . . . .

. . . .

8. . . . .

. . . .

9. . . . .

. . . .

10. . . . .

. . . .

AUTISTIC PRIDE

It is important to like and value yourself and reject any thought that you and your autism need to be 'fixed'. This idea of liking and valuing yourself when you are an autistic person is often called 'Autistic Pride'.

Autistic Pride is a very good thing and means that we feel good about being ourselves, without feeling like we have to change who we are.

The idea of 'pride' might seem a bit confusing. Some people might think that it is odd to be 'proud' of something you cannot help and didn't really 'do' – such as being autistic. Autistic Pride is actually very different to being proud of doing a good job at something. It isn't like bragging or having a big ego either. Autistic Pride is about knowing that you can be true to yourself. You could think to yourself:

I like me for who I am. Being autistic is part of me and is nothing to be ashamed of. In fact I am very happy and proud to be my awesome autistic self!

Autistic Pride is about you being happy to be who you are, whatever anyone else says. It might take a bit of practice and time to feel that way. This is perfectly fine. Some people feel proud to be autistic the day they find out they are autistic, and some people take much longer. There is no one right way to 'do' Autistic Pride.

Some other groups in society have the same sort of ideas about Pride. People who are lesbian, gay, bi, transgender, intersex, queer and/or asexual (sometimes shortened to LGBTIQA) have been talking about the idea of Pride in their community for a long time.

AM I DIFFERENT? YES, I AM!

A strength that autistic people often have is simply that we are quite different to most of the other people in the world. It's worth reading that sentence again because it's important. Being different is a STRENGTH. We think differently, see things differently and understand the world differently. Being different might seem like a bad thing or something you don't like about yourself. In fact, being different is very important and is often a very good thing. The natural world encourages diversity in the gene pool because it makes the whole population stronger.

The world needs all sorts of different people to work well. Imagine if everyone had the same interests and the same strengths. Imagine if everyone was interested in making and performing music. The world would have an amazing soundtrack, but there would be no farmers or bus drivers or scientists or researchers. A world like that wouldn't do very well! Our world needs people with different skills and interests and strengths to make it work. Autistic people have some incredible skills and knowledge to contribute. If we weren't different, if we didn't have passions for a topic and we didn't have our strong focus, our loyalty and kindness, and the other qualities we tend to have, then the world would miss out on all those good things.

Autistic people have different skills and interests

It is likely that many really important people in history who have made big breakthroughs in areas like science and mathematics, music and art may well have been autistic. Without those people, the world we live in now would be very different.

Not everyone understands how important it is to have a lot of different people with different skills and ways of thinking and doing things. Some people are mean and rude to people who are different. When people are mean to us because of our differences, it is actually the person being mean who has got this totally wrong. It is important to know that if someone picks on you for being different or for being autistic, the other person is the one who is wrong, and not you.

Liking, loving and respecting yourself are really great things. It can sometimes be difficult to do this, but it makes life a lot happier. It is also true that other people need to treat you with respect too. Every single person deserves respect from their fellow human beings – no matter how old or young they are, whatever their gender, wherever they or their family come from or whether they are autistic or not.

ACTIVITY: Write down some things about you that are awesome

These might be things you enjoy doing, or things you are good at, or things about your personality and who you are. You can write down lots of things or just one or two – it's up to you.

1. ....

....

2. ....

....

3. ....

....

4. ....

....

5. ....

....

6. ....

....

7. ....

....

8. ....

....

9. ....

....

10. ....

....

Chapter 4

Why Being You Can Sometimes Be Hard

In the last chapter, we talked about strengths that autistic people often have. Just like every person has strengths, every person also has challenges, or things they find difficult. Not every autistic person is the same, but there are quite a few things that many of us find difficult.

SENSORY DIFFERENCES

We have eight different senses our brain uses to get information from the world and our bodies:

- Sight

- Sound

- Smell

- Taste

- Touch

- Interoceptive

- Proprioceptive

- Vestibular.

Most people haven't heard of the last three, so we'll tell you a bit about them. They give us information about what is happening inside our body or how our body is moving. You might feel dizzy if you spin too much. That's our vestibular system working. It's interesting to know that it works using special canals and tiny organs inside our ears, so our ears are very busy little things! Our vestibular system helps us balance and stay upright when we walk. You might find it very relaxing to swing or sway in a hammock. That is also your vestibular system working.

Some autistic people like to feel squeezed or to have a weight on them. That is our proprioceptive system, which is made up of sensors inside our muscles sending messages to our brain. We can sometimes find it very calming to do an activity that gives what we call 'deep pressure'. There are lots of ways to do this, like a weighted blanket, or swimming.

Our interoceptive system gives our brain information about how our organs are feeling, like when we need to eat or go to the toilet. For some autistic people, our interoceptive system needs a bit of help to work well or it might take a bit longer to develop. That's totally fine.

Autistic people often experience messages from our senses in a different way. Sometimes sounds are extra-loud for us, or smells or tastes are extra-strong, or the seam or tag in our shirt is very painful. It's so much better when clothes have labels printed on the inside of the fabric instead of a flap of scratchy material!

One of us (the authors) really hates fungus and finds the smell so strong and horrible that they had to go right away from someone who was having a mushroom omelette. The fungus smell was completely overpowering until the omelette was all eaten. We both often wear noise-cancelling head-phones at work, to listen to music and block out all the office conversations. We take them off for meetings. A friend of ours is very sensitive to light and wears a cap all the time. This is all fine too.

Sometimes everyday noises are too loud for us

Sometimes it can be hard for non-autistic people to understand how strong sensory input can be for us, especially when it comes to food. Eating involves all our senses. There might be foods we like the textures, tastes or smells of, and foods that we don't. Some of us just find a few different meals we like and eat those all the time. There is nothing wrong with that, as long as we get the nutrition we need. Sometimes as we get older, it is easier to try new and different foods and find some other options. In the meantime, we can have supplements or special drinks that have a lot of vitamins, minerals and protein in them, so our bodies get what they need.

MELTDOWNS

You might have heard people talk about meltdowns. The first thing we need to tell you is that a meltdown is not something you can control. It is NOT your fault. If anyone tries to tell you it is, or punishes you for having a meltdown, show them this chapter! It's also very different from having a tantrum, like toddlers can have if they don't get what they want.

A meltdown can be different for different people. Some autistic people feel like they have a lot of energy that they need to get rid of. We might yell or feel like we need to kick and punch things to release that energy. And some autistic people go very quiet, need to be alone and can't talk to anybody. Sometimes that is called a 'shutdown'.

We have meltdowns or shutdowns because our brains have been overloaded. That might be from too much sensory input, like being in a loud, crowded shopping mall. Or it might be from too much social interaction if we don't like being around groups of people we don't know, or even people we DO know, or some other activity that we find stressful. We can call these things 'triggers'.

What are some of your triggers? We have started a list that might help.

Trigger	Where could this happen?
Lots of people talking at once	Classroom, schoolyard/ playground, shopping mall
Smells we don't like	Public toilets, perfume counters at shops, public transport

Sometimes it can be hard to know what has caused a meltdown and it's often one last little thing on top of many other things. The trick is to take some of the stress away before it gets to that point. Imagine your brain is like a soft drink bottle. Each time you experience a trigger, it's like someone shaking the soft drink bottle and the pressure from the gas gradually builds a bit more, until the lid is ready to pop off.

If we can take some time to do something relaxing, or escape from the triggers, it is like opening the lid of the bottle very slowly and letting some of the gas out with a 'fffffffffff' sound. The drink stays in the bottle and the pressure is very gently released.

We will talk about some strategies to help you do this in Chapter 5.

SOCIAL DIFFERENCES

One thing autistic people often find difficult is figuring out how people feel just by listening to their voices and looking at their facial expressions and body language. You might hear some people who should know better say that autistic people have no 'empathy'. Empathy means the ability to understand and share how other people feel.

There are lots of different kinds of empathy. One kind is being able to work out how people feel by listening to and looking at them. That is the kind that we can sometimes find hard.

One other kind of empathy is being able to share and understand someone's feelings once we know how they feel. We often have a LOT of that kind of empathy, even more than non-autistic people. The trick is to find out how people feel. Sometimes it is obvious – if they are crying, they are probably sad. But sometimes it is not obvious and often we can just ask them! If a friend tells you about something that has happened to them, you can just say something like, 'How did that make you feel?'

You might find that autistic people tend to be a lot more straightforward in their communication. We say what we mean, and we mean what we say. Sometimes it seems like non-autistic people are speaking a different language, with hidden meanings. You might find it easier to communicate with other autistic people, so it's really helpful to find some autistic friends, especially ones who share the same passions and interests that you do! We talk a bit about that in the next chapter.

Another difference that we often have is how we feel about the truth. Most autistic people are very honest, which is a VERY good thing! But some non-autistic people don't like hearing the truth or being corrected, and think feelings are more important than truth. They can be upset if we tell them something truthful that they don't want to hear. Often to us, it's just information, and not linked to whether we like the person or not. A silly example is someone saying, 'Does my bottom look big in this?' A non-autistic person would probably say, 'No, of course not' (even if it did), because the person asking does not want to be told they have a big bottom. An autistic person might say, 'Yes, it does', because we tell the truth.

This can be an important difference to be aware of when being around your friends. If you're ever unsure of what to say, it's useful to bounce the question back to them. They will often give you a list of possible responses.

BULLYING

Very sadly, some autistic people get bullied at school and other places. There are some people in the world who don't like anyone who is different from them. How boring, wanting everyone to just be like them! It's taking time to change, but there are many people who are working very hard on fixing this problem.

It's very important to remember that it is ALWAYS the fault of the bully, not the person being bullied. Often, people who are bullies feel very bad about themselves underneath. It's like they need to hurt other people to feel better about themselves. But this is completely wrong and never works.

Bullying was easier to manage when we (the authors) were teenagers because we didn't have social media. Any bullying finished when you got home after school. So it's important to be safe online and there are lots of ways to help you do this, such as not using your real name, not giving out personal details, being careful about what you share and not being friends with people unless you know (and like!) them in real life. Having a trusted group of friends, even if they are adults or people you don't go to school with, helps as well.

Whatever anyone says, bullying is NOT your fault and you do not need to try and fix it by yourself. If you ever feel like you've been bullied, speak to a trusted teacher or other adult and tell them what is happening.

ANXIETY

Not all autistic people feel anxious, but many of us do, and we feel anxious about different things. Sometimes it makes us feel angry or worried. We might say angry things we would not normally say.

One thing many of us don't like is not knowing what is going to happen when we go somewhere new. That can be hard when we want to go on a school camp, for example, or maybe start a new job. Something that can help is to find out as much as we can before we do the new thing. You can search online to find out what it looks like, look at a satellite map, read about the facilities, who is going to be there, maybe even have a short visit beforehand, to try and reduce what you don't know about it. The more we know about what is going to happen, the less we have to worry about, and the more comfortable we feel.

When you were younger, someone might have shown you a social story before you had a new experience. Social stories are short stories with pictures about what is going to happen. An example is what will happen on a visit to the dentist. As we get older, we can make our own social stories by doing our own research.

There are also many health professionals, like psychologists or counsellors, who can help you build strategies to reduce anxiety.

BEING ORGANIZED

Some autistic people find it challenging to plan and organize things. This isn't so hard in primary school because there is a lot less to remember – one room, often one teacher, and not as much homework. It gets harder in high school or secondary school with more subjects, rooms, teachers and homework. But there are lots of planning tools to use – electronic ones or paper ones on a wall, a diary, or more than one method if you prefer. You might find it helpful to colour-code your books for different subjects (if you have books that are not digital), and have your class and assignment timetables colour-coded the same way.

It can be tricky to stay on top of assignments that need to be done outside of school, especially if it's a subject you don't like that much. You might hate maths. Or you might not like English. People often put things off when they don't like to do them. But we often don't feel good when we have a task just sitting and waiting for us to do until the last minute. It always feels much better to have it done and you can learn to reward yourself by doing something you like: 'I will write 250 words of this essay, then I will game for 30 minutes' or something like that. Or maybe you like to do it all in one go.

It's also helpful to get into the habit of using your phone or other device to monitor important dates, with reminders. This is something you might need to do as an adult. You might have a shared family electronic diary, so everyone can support each other to get their tasks done on time.

In the next chapter, we talk about some strategies that can help to make life a bit easier.

⇒ Chapter 5 ⇐

Some Ways to Make Life Easier

The world we live in can be very confusing for autistic people. There are many things we find easy to understand, but some 'social' type things are difficult for us (although we are expected to just know and understand them anyway). Sometimes it can feel like we are on a different planet! It can be hard to make ourselves understood. Things can seem to happen all at once and we might have a meltdown or a shutdown. Sometimes we might find something very stressful or upsetting that doesn't seem to worry anyone else, like a school assembly with hundreds of kids who all smell different listening to a school band playing a little bit out of tune.

The good news is that there are loads of things autistic people can do to make life easier.

EVERYDAY LIFE

As all autistic people are different, something that works for one person might not work for another. Even so, there are some things that lots of autistic people find make the world easier to live in. A few things that might help you are as follows.

At school

You could use your passions to start a lunchtime club at school. This means you are likely to meet people who are interested in the same things as you. A coding or gaming club, a writing club or an art club are easy to set up, and teachers enjoy working with students who are passionate about something. This can be a place where you make friends or find people who share what you really love. It can be a lot easier to talk to other kids if you share an interest with them. A club at lunchtime also means you will not need to be in the schoolyard/playground at lunchtime. Quite a lot of autistic kids dislike being in the schoolyard/playground for a number of reasons.

Have some communication cards to use at school, especially if too much is going on and making you stressed and scared, so that it is difficult to communicate. These cards have emotions written on them, so you can show them to your teacher if you can't actually say what you are feeling in words. You can download some to use or make your own. Keep them on a keyring on your desk or somewhere close by so they are easy to reach and show your teacher. For example, there are Minecraft cards online that communicate how you are feeling, right from feeling totally calm like Steve, to feeling a bit explosive like a Creeper, right up to a lava card, meaning, 'I need to leave right now'. It is a good idea to have this card signed by your principal or headteacher.

Some autistic kids need changes made to the classroom to make school easier. These include things like:

- Having breaks from the classroom

- Choosing where to sit

- Skipping noisy activities

- Having sensory aides in class, like therapy putty or elastic bands on chair legs to press legs against

- Having a quiet space to go to de-stress

- Working alone instead of in a group

■ Doing homework in a different way, such as changing the topic of an assignment, or making a slide presentation instead of doing a talk.

Autistic kids are usually allowed to have these changes in the classroom. You may already have something like this but, if you don't, you can talk to your parent or carer or teacher about what might make school easier for you to manage. It is the law that schools have to make these changes for you so, if they don't, talk to your parent or carer about it. There are people who can help if your school is not supporting you in the way it should.

When something is difficult

If something is happening or has happened that you find upsetting, tell a parent or carer or an adult you trust. You do not need to go through life alone fixing all the problems you come across.

Likewise, if you have questions about what is going on in your life, ask a parent or carer or another adult you trust. Adults have usually had more experience and might have answers to questions you think are impossible.

Talk about when something is too loud, too bright or too smelly, and tell your parent or carer to ask for it to be changed, or ask yourself. One of us (TM) worked with a woman who put strong-smelling oils on herself. TM found the oils so strong and smelly that it made her eyes water, but the woman could barely smell them. The woman was very happy to stop once she knew how much it bothered TM.

It is important to know that sometimes it won't be possible to change something, even if you or your parent or carer ask. If this happens, you can talk to your parent or carer about some ways that you can work around the sensory nasties without getting rid of them.

In life

Find some autistic friends or interest groups. These can be online or in 'real' life. We both spend a lot of time communicating with other autistic people. Spending time with other autistic kids is often a great thing, and you may well find you have common interests.

Spend time on your passionate interests. Chances are this will make you very happy. This is one of the many gifts of autism – to be delighted by working on things we are passionate about.

Remember that your thoughts and ideas and your likes and dislikes are as important as everybody else's.

Tell yourself nice and positive things about yourself. Do this often. If you have trouble thinking of what you are good at, then talk to a parent or carer or another adult you trust about this. They may well know a lot of good things about you that you are not aware of.

This can be a tricky one, but try not to change how you act in front of people to make yourself seem more like them and less like you. Autistic people can be pressured to act 'less autistic', but we ARE autistic, and we are good people just as we are. This might be a difficult thing to do as there can be a lot of pressure to act like everyone else, but try to remind yourself that there is nothing 'wrong' with you and you are great as you are, as a wonderful autistic person.

As you go through life you will learn more things that make your life easier. These are often called 'strategies' and each different person has different strategies that work for them. You can talk to a parent or carer, a supportive adult, an autistic friend or a health professional about what they think helps you and what you find helpful. This is a list of things that will keep growing as you get older.

HELPING WITH MELTDOWNS AND SHUTDOWNS

One very common experience for autistic people — kids and adults alike — is overload and meltdowns or shutdowns, which we talked about in the previous chapter. Here, we talk about some things that can help.

Many autistic people can feel when a meltdown or shutdown is about to happen and can take steps to 'de-escalate'. It's helpful to think very hard about these things, because no one likes having meltdowns, and we often feel very tired afterwards. But it can be difficult to know how stressed we are just by how we feel. You might feel hot, or prickly, or start to feel shaky, or your limbs might feel a bit stiff, like a robot. Everyone feels different. And sometimes we are in a public place and don't feel comfortable to let out all our energy, so we keep it inside until we are somewhere safe. That's okay, but we do need to let it out at some point.

Learning about what you can do to help gently release some of that pressure before the lid from the soft drink bottle pops off and you have a meltdown or shutdown is extremely helpful. You do not need to do this alone and you can talk to your parent or carer, an autistic adult you might know or a health professional about learning how to 'de-escalate'.

Spending time with animals can help us feel calm

You might already do some things to gently release some pressure and help you to calm down.

Some of the things autistic kids do to help when they are getting overwhelmed include:

- Reading in a tent or other quiet place

- Gaming with headphones on

- Sitting or lying under a weighted blanket or weighted toy

- Playing with pets or spending time with other animals if you have no pets

- Baking

- Doing art

- Walking around in nature

- Sorting your crystal collection (or whatever collection you have)

- Doing something active to release energy, like jumping on a trampoline or punching a punching bag

- Being in a quiet, calm place.

This table shows some of the things that might make you 'fizz' and turn into a meltdown or shutdown, and some of the things that might help you calm down. Add some more if you like.

Stressful thing	Calming strategy
Too much noise/people	Time in a quiet space with headphones on. If you can't leave, put noise-cancelling headphones on and read or play some games on a device
Argument with sibling, or another kid at school	Stay away from the person you argued with and don't talk to anyone until you feel calmer
Frustration at making a mistake or not doing a good job at something	Stop doing the thing you are frustrated about. Do something else that you enjoy. Remember, FAIL stands for First Attempt In Learning. You can always try again another time
Sensory nasties – bad smells, bright lights, loud noises and other sensory things	Either get away from the source of the problem or find something to help manage it – like wearing a baseball cap when there are glary lights or carrying something you like the smell of. A citrus oil can work well
Worrying and 'overthinking'	Do something you enjoy and don't find stressful. This can help to stop your brain from worrying. You can also talk to a parent or carer or trusted adult about what is worrying you as well and they may be able to help. Health professionals such as psychologists can also help with this

Stressful thing	Calming strategy

Stressful thing	Calming strategy

As you grow older, you will find it easier to know how many triggers or stressful things you can manage before you need some 'me time'. For example, if you have been invited to a party on a Saturday that you want to go to, you might need to have a quiet night on Friday and a relaxing day doing things you like on Sunday. It's a bit like money. Having 'me time' is like putting money in the bank. Doing something difficult is like spending money. Spending money is fine if you have the money in the bank first.

It's important to have some 'me time'

WHAT IS STIMMING AND WHY IS IT A GOOD THING?

Stimming is a word that means a number of different activities that autistic people do in order to feel calmer or when we are really happy. Stims include flapping hands, clicking fingers, playing with material or fidget toys and rocking. Stims often make us feel really good and can make a big difference and help when we are stressed or anxious. Some people think stimming is bad thing because it can make us look a bit odd. In fact, stimming is a positive thing and if people have a problem with it, it is they who need to learn to be a bit more accepting and respectful. Every autistic person has their own stims that work for them. Some people have stims that are really noisy. If this is something you do it is okay to have noisy stims, but you need to make sure you are not hurting other people's ears. It is best to not be too close to other people when you do it.

ACTIVITY: Do you have any stims? What are they?

1. ....

....

2. ....

....

3. ....

....

4. ....

....

5. ....

....

6. ....

....

7. ....

....

8. ....

....

9. ....

....

10. ....

....

COMMUNICATION

Some autistic people do not use verbal speech.
They might use an iPad or a special device for
communication. Some people speak sometimes and
not at other times, and some people don't speak at
all. It is okay if you don't speak. Some people think
that if you don't speak you have nothing to say, but
this is definitely not the case! Communicating is
all about people understanding what you say and
you understanding what they say. It doesn't matter
how that communication is done – if it is through
typing or sign language or speaking or using
pictures or using a device.

There are lots of ways to communicate

SOME TIPS AND THOUGHTS FROM OTHER AUTISTIC KIDS

SAMARA

Autism is like a fabulous long dress. It adds a lot to you but sometimes it trips you up.

LUKE – 'STAY WHO YOU ARE'

If you get bullied because of who you are, it doesn't mean you should change. It's better to stay who you are.

SUMMER – 'BEING DIFFERENT IS GREAT!'

Some people will always find a way to pick on the person who is different. Be strong. Being different is great!

ABBY – 'HOW I DEALT WITH THE CHANGE THIS YEAR'

I get very stressed about a lot of things but change and doing new things is the absolute worst one. Every time I start a new year at school I get really worried because I will have to have a new teacher and meet other kids. Last summer I thought that I didn't like all the change at school. I had sort of always known this inside me but I had never really thought about it making me stressed before. Sometimes I can't really feel when I'm stressed. I told my dad and he said he would do what he could to help. My dad talked to my school and I got to meet my new teacher about a month before school started and I met her a few more times after that. She told me all about what I would be learning. I also got to have a look at the classroom. I was still really scared and worried about starting the new year but it was much better than before. Now I know that I can work on this next year as well. And next year is a big change because I am going to high school [secondary school] then. But I feel a bit better about it because of how I dealt with the change this year.

KY – 'IT STINKS!'

I really hate strong smells. I wouldn't go to the toilet at school for about a year because it stank. I really couldn't go in. I would hold on all day. This would make me anxious and it felt very uncomfortable. I didn't think it was something I could talk about – it is embarrassing! My teacher noticed I wasn't going to the bathroom and asked me why. I told him it stinks and I couldn't go in so he talked to the other teachers and they said I could use the toilet in the staff room which has fewer people using it, so while it is still smelly, I can actually go in there. It is much better now.

VINH – 'IT [THE LUNCHTIME BOOK CLUB] WAS THE BEST THING EVER!!'

I used to hate being in the schoolyard [playground] at lunchtime and recess [break time]. It was confusing with kids going everywhere and it was always when I would get bullied. I usually just tried to find a quiet corner and read. Just a few weeks ago one of the teachers said there will be a lunchtime book club for kids who like reading. I went the first time it was on and it was the BEST thing EVER!! It has a teacher there so it is safe from bullies and you just go there and read a book. It is every day except for Friday so now, every day except for Friday, I go to book club and read books. Some kids talk to each other at book club. I haven't really done that as I am happy with my books, but it is a very cool thing to do at lunchtime.

ACTIVITY: Write down your own tips and ideas

Here is a place where you can write in some things you use to make your life easier:

1. ....

....

2. ....

....

3. ....

....

4. ....

....

5. ....

....

6. ....

....

7. ....

....

8. ....

....

9. ....

....

10. ....

....

⇕ Chapter 6 ⇖

Growing Up True to You

There are a number of things that can happen as people grow older — things like changes in friendships, puberty and thinking about gender identity. These can be challenging or confusing for autistic people, but they do not need to be scary. Knowing some information about these topics can help make them less confusing.

GENDER DIVERSITY

Gender is complex. It involves how we experience our own bodies, how we feel inside and how we express ourselves to the world. Some people think that there are just female and male, it's how you were born, and that's it. But that's not right and it's not helpful.

Many autistic people are trans and gender diverse. Gender diversity includes being transgender, non-binary, gender-fluid and many other different sorts of gender identities. Being trans and gender diverse is perfectly okay. People who are trans and gender diverse often feel like the gender on their birth certificate is different from what they feel like. Many people try different ways of expressing their gender and this is okay. They might wear different clothes or use a different name that they feel fits them better than the one on their birth certificate. Autistic people are actually more likely to be trans and gender diverse than everyone else. One of the authors of this book is non-binary gender, and the autistic writer and academic Dr Wenn Lawson, who is quoted in this book, is transgender.

You may have had some thoughts about how you feel about your gender or you might not. Some people have unhelpful views about gender diversity and think it is wrong to be gender diverse. In fact, it is these people who are wrong. Being trans and gender diverse is nothing to be ashamed of or embarrassed about. Questioning your gender is a natural thing for many people to do. If you are questioning your gender it is a good idea to talk to someone about it. It is usually best to talk to a trusted adult such as a parent or carer or relative you feel close to. You might also tell your friends. Who you tell and whether you tell anyone is completely up to you.

Some people know very clearly that they are trans and gender diverse and other people may have questions but not be certain. There are no wrong answers when it comes to gender diversity. Each person's views mean something to them and that is okay. Some people think about and question their gender when they are kids or teens, and other people do not do so until they are adults. Others never question their gender identity at all. All of these options are perfectly okay.

People who are trans and gender diverse often have similar feelings about their sense of identity and who they are as people do about being autistic. Many trans and gender diverse people feel very proud to be who they are.

PUBERTY

Puberty is a stage of development that happens to people at different ages, but usually somewhere between 9 and 13 years. You may have experienced puberty, or maybe not yet. It involves some physical changes to your body, getting to know yourself, and often changes to how people think, such as being interested in having a relationship. Puberty is a big topic and there is not really enough room in this book to go into much detail other than this brief introduction. There are other books that give lots of detailed information. Puberty is all about you getting more mature and changing from a child into an adult. It can be helpful to talk to a parent or carer or trusted adult about puberty, especially if you are worried about it. If you are trans and gender diverse, puberty can be a very difficult time. If this is you, then it is a good idea to talk to a parent or carer or trusted adult so you can work through any issues together.

FRIENDSHIPS

You might have a friend or more than one friend. Friendships can be a wonderful thing. Friends often share interests, can be supportive of each other and enjoy spending time together. As you get older you might notice some changes in your friendships. People who are autistic and those who are not can have different experiences in terms of what they are interested in as they grow older. You might find that any friends you have who are not autistic suddenly start being interested in different sorts of things to you. They might be interested in relationships with other people or music or films they weren't interested in before. This can leave autistic kids feeling left out. This is a difficult thing, but it is not necessarily because your friends don't like you anymore. It is more likely to happen because autistic people and non-autistic people can sometimes mature differently. It doesn't mean autistic kids are any worse or better than our non-autistic friends and peers, just different.

And on the topic of friends, sometimes people we think are our friends behave in a way that isn't very friendly. They might be competitive or mean and sometimes even act like bullies. People like this aren't usually friends at all, and you are better off without them. Some of the ways to spot a 'real' friend are:

- They are friendly towards you

- They share interests with you

- You enjoy being with them

- They share things with you, such as outings, games, toys or jokes

- They don't make fun of you or put you down in front of other people

- They say nice things to and about you

- They 'get' you.

YOU ARE IN CONTROL OF YOUR BODY

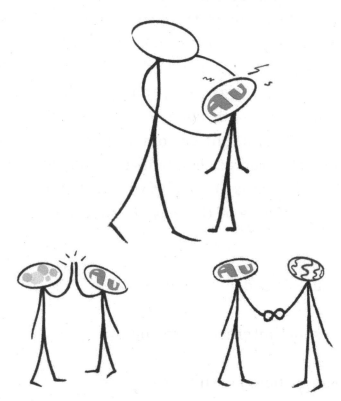

**You can say 'no thanks' to a hug. You might prefer a high
five or fist bump. No physical contact at all is fine too**

This is a really important part of the book, all
about the fact that you decide what you do – and
what others do – with your body. The fact that you
are in control of your own body is probably fairly
obvious. You are the person who decides what your
body does after all! Where things get a bit more
complicated is when it comes to what other people
do to your body. Just like you are in control of what
you decide to do with your own body, you also have

the right to say what other people can and can't do with your body. If someone wants to give you a hug and you don't want them to, you can ask them not to and they should listen to your wishes. If someone else says they don't want you to do something with their body, like giving them a hug, you need to respect their wishes and not do the thing that they don't want you to.

Where this can get difficult is if the other person does not listen to what you want. A really important thing to know is that people should not touch your body without your permission. Even if it is a doctor or a teacher, they should ask your permission before touching you. You have the right to say no to people touching you, but if it is a doctor or other health worker (like a nurse) they might need to touch your body as part of medical treatment. In this situation you should have a parent or carer or trusted adult with you when the medical treatment is happening.

If anyone other than a doctor or health worker wants to touch your body or make you do something with your body, you can say yes or no. If someone tries to touch your body or make you do something with your body without your permission and continues to do so after you tell them no, then get away from them if you can, and tell a trusted adult.

The same thing applies when other people want you to do things with their bodies. If someone tells you to do something with their body and you do not want to, then you do not have to.

This idea about being in control of your body is called *body autonomy* and it is very important to make sure nobody does anything to you against your wishes.

⇒ Chapter 7 ⇐

Telling Others About Your Autism

Some autistic people are very open about being autistic. We (the authors) are. Other autistic people prefer to keep it to themselves and that's okay too. It's totally up to you whether you'd like to tell lots of people, just a few close friends and your teachers, or no one. Your parent or carer will probably tell your school, so that your teacher knows how to work best with you. That's a good thing.

Unfortunately, sometimes people are prejudiced against something they don't understand. This happens with different cultures, religions, gender diversity — all sorts of things. Often, the best way to handle that sort of prejudice is to be open and honest. That is why there are lots of autistic people called advocates who work hard at helping other people understand what autism is all about. Some of those people are mentioned in Chapter 2, like Summer, Cadence and Dr Wenn. Yenn (one of the authors of this book) has written lots of books about autism and travels around Australia talking about autism to medical professionals, teachers, parents, carers and many other people.

Another reason to be open about your autism is that people might have wrong beliefs about autism, like we spoke about in Chapter 1. Also, every autistic person is different, so what people think they know about autism may not apply to you. They might think all autistic people are excellent at maths and want you to help them with their homework. But you might HATE maths so you wouldn't want to do that at all!

Perhaps you spend time with someone like an occupational therapist or psychologist who helps you to develop strategies to overcome challenges in your life. It's important to be as open and honest as you can with those people, so they can help you. It's not easy to talk about things we find difficult, but it's the best way to get the support we sometimes need.

Sometimes parents or carers talk about their children to doctors and therapists as if the child is not right there, listening. That can make us feel invisible and unimportant, especially if they are talking about things we find difficult. A good strategy is to prepare a list of things we find challenging and give that to the doctor or therapist to read, so they can think about strategies to help. This is often much easier than talking about it, including for people who use speech to communicate. Or you might like to wait outside the doctor's or therapist's room with a book or device while your parent or carer goes in and talks with the doctor or therapist first.

Just remember, it is YOUR autism and you have the right to be included in discussions about it. You can choose whether you would like to be included or not.

TYLER

I always hated going to psychologist appointments with my mum. Sometimes they would talk about me like I wasn't there. I felt awful when they were talking about a meltdown I had when it was way too noisy and I didn't have my headphones. So I asked them to please stop talking about me like I wasn't there. I think they were a bit surprised. I was surprised, too, when they listened to me and understood. Now I talk to the psychologist on my own and mum waits outside. Sometimes I need to talk about private things now that I am getting older.

TELLING PEOPLE AT SCHOOL

We won't lie – people can be unkind sometimes, and some schools have a culture that is more supportive than others. We hope you have a supportive school! But a good way to overcome stereotypes and myths and to ensure your classmates understand YOUR autism is to talk about it. It also stops your classmates wondering why you might skip noisy activities or be away from school on sports competition days or wear noise-cancelling headphones in class when they aren't allowed to.

When people don't know the reason for something, they often come up with their own theories. And they are often wrong! Think about how many silly theories there have been in the past, like diseases being spread by a bad smell instead of germs. People used to carry a bundle of herbs that smelled nice to keep the disease away! Now we know that this is a very silly theory, but back then, people didn't know any better.

You might find it helpful to prepare a small slide show for your class, or a handout. It could include things like:

- What is autism?

- What is autism NOT?

- Your strengths

- Your challenges

- What classmates can do to be supportive.

This book might be helpful in giving you some ideas of what to include.

Talking about your autism can help people understand

Another strategy is to have some answers ready for common questions like, 'What does autism mean?' or 'How does autism make you different?'

SAMARA

Sometimes people ask me why I leave school early every day or why I'm not there sometimes. I tell them that I'm autistic and that means school is a bit harder for me. Some people ask, 'What's that?' I just tell them my brain works differently from most people's and school is stressful. No one has ever been mean to me about being autistic.

People can sometimes think that being autistic means you need help with everything. We all know that is not true. Like everyone, we need support with some things and there are many, many other things we can do on our own. Sometimes we might need to say something like, 'Thanks for your help, but I am fine to do this on my own.' We can always ask someone if we do need help, just like everyone does.

It is important to remember that you are growing up to be an independent adult and you can choose who knows about your autism and what to tell them about it.

You have nearly reached the end of this book! But we just need one more chapter about how awesome you are.

Chapter 8

Big Yay for Being You!

'Autistic' by Samara

Atypical
Unlike most others
Terrifically different
Insightful
Sensory superstars
Totally authentic
Interests are STRONG
Changing the world

Do you agree with Samara's acrostic poem about what it means to be autistic? Are there other things you would say about being autistic? There are no right or wrong answers to this. Have a think. You can write down your thoughts if you like, or just keep them inside your head if you prefer.

ACTIVITY: My thoughts about being autistic

1. . . . .

. . . .

2. . . . .

. . . .

3. . . . .

. . . .

4. . . . .

. . . .

5. . . . .

. . . .

6. . . . .

. . . .

7. . . . .

. . . .

8. . . . .

. . . .

9. . . . .

. . . .

10. . . . .

. . . .

We have looked at a lot of things in this book, and you might not remember everything. You might come back and read it again. But for now, remember this one extremely important point: autistic people matter and autism is a different – but just as valid – way that people process and respond to the world.

Everyone has strengths and interests. All the parts of being autistic go towards making you the unique person that you are. You are a wonderful part of what makes up the world, and your autism is a big part of what makes you 'you'!

As we have seen in this book, being autistic isn't always easy. People in the world can be horrible and some things – like change and sensory nasties and meltdowns – can make life really difficult too. Hopefully having read this book you will have more of an idea of what being autistic means for you. You might also have learned some useful tips to make your life easier. You might have more knowledge of how you fit into the world and how there are lots of other autistic people in the world who might be a bit like you. *You are definitely not alone!*

ACTIVITY: What is your favourite thing (or things) about being you?

This could be something you do well or that you are really interested in or it could just be part of what makes you who you are.

1. . . . .

. . . .

2. . . . .

. . . .

3. . . . .

. . . .

4. . . . .

. . . .

5. ....

....

6. ....

....

7. ....

....

8. ....

....

9. ....

....

10. ....

....

ACTIVITY: Some of the things that help make you who you are

Your name: . . . .

Your age: . . . .

Passionate interest/s:

. . . .

. . . .

. . . .

. . . .

Favourite colour:

. . . .

Best fandom:

. . . .

Best game:

. . . .

Avatar or cosplay name and character (if you have one):

. . . .

. . . .

Favourite book:

. . . .

Favourite toy:

. . . .

Food you love:

. . . .

. . . .

. . . .

Food you don't love:

. . . .

. . . .

. . . .

Pets' names (if you have pets):

. . . .

. . . .

. . . .

What you like about your pets:

. . . .

. . . .

. . . .

Anything you would like to learn:

. . . .

. . . .

. . . .

What device/s you use:

. . . .

Best film/s:

. . . .

. . . .

. . . .

Favourite musician/band:

. . . .

. . . .

Best stim:

. . . .

. . . .

Favourite picture/painting:

. . . .

. . . .

You are your own wonderful, individual, autistic self. The things you like and enjoy are part of that. You are amazing and the world is a better place because you are in it. You have every right to be a proud autistic person and to be happy to be yourself.

We hope that you have found this book helpful in exploring YOUR autism. Every autistic person is different, like every person in the world is different (and quite probably aliens anywhere in the universe too). Sometimes it is hard to be different, but nature encourages difference – it is a great thing!

Like many others we know, *you are an actually awesome autistic person. Keep being you!*